Ducks

Jennifer Szymanski

NATIONAL GEOGRAPHIC

Washington, D.C.

Vocabulary Tree

ANIMALS

DUCKS

WHAT THEY HAVE

beaks
webbed feet
feathers
wings

WHAT THEY DO

get food
fly
swim
waddle

WHERE THEY LIVE

pond
marsh
ocean
lake

mallard

This is a duck.

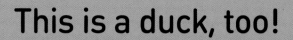

This is a duck, too!

mandarin duck

blue-winged teal

There are many
kinds of ducks.

All ducks are

alike in many ways.

All ducks have beaks.

ruddy duck

hooded merganser

They use their beaks
to get food.

Ducks have webbed feet.
They use their feet to swim.

They use their feet
to waddle, too.

Ducks have feathers and wings.

Feathers keep them warm and dry. Wings help them fly.

Steller's eider

All ducks live near water.

comb ducks

Some ducks live
by a pond.

Some ducks live in a marsh.

lesser
whistling-duck

surf scoters

Other ducks live
by the ocean.

Some ducks fly to a new place

when it gets cold out.

mallards

They come back
when it is warm!

mallards

Then they start
a new family.

Migration

Many ducks migrate (MY-grate). Ducks that migrate fly to another place for part of the year. Sometimes they fly a long way! This map shows the paths that some ducks in North America take when they migrate.

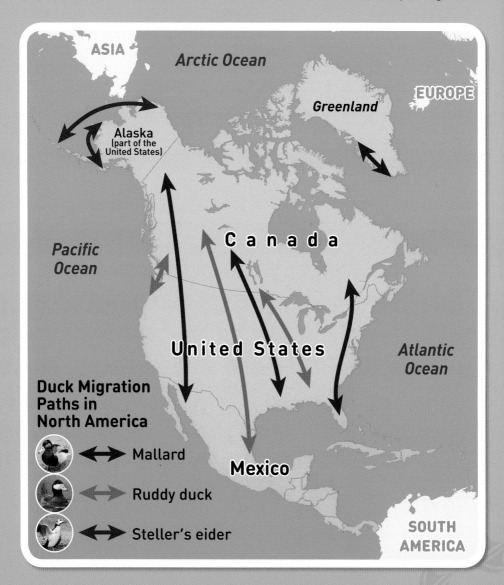

ASIA

Arctic Ocean

EUROPE

Greenland

Alaska
(part of the
United States)

Pacific
Ocean

C a n a d a

U n i t e d   S t a t e s

Atlantic
Ocean

Mexico

Duck Migration
Paths in
North America

Mallard

Ruddy duck

Steller's eider

SOUTH
AMERICA

Draw a duck. What body parts does it have? What is it doing?

To my mom —J.S.

The author and publisher gratefully acknowledge the expert content review of this book by Dr. Gary Hepp, Emeritus Professor, School of Forestry and Wildlife Sciences, Auburn University, and the literacy review of this book by Kimberly Gillow, Principal, Milan Area Schools, Michigan.

Designed by Anne LeongSon

Photo Credits

GI=Getty Images; MP=Minden Pictures; SS=Shutterstock

Cover, shuchunke/GI; 1, Tom Reichner/SS; 2-3, sh.el.photo/SS; 4, Westbury/GI; 5, Tze-hsin Woo/GI; 6-7, George Grall/National Geographic Creative; 8, Glenn Bartley/GI; 9, Steve Gettle/MP; 10, Michael Krabs/imagebroker/ARDEA; 11, Joesboy/GI; 12-13, Hugh Harrop/Alamy Stock Photo; 14-15, Ron O'Connor/MP; 16, Hanne and Jens Eriksen/MP; 17, Vicki Jauron, Babylon and Beyond Photography/GI; 18-19, mirceax/GI; 20-21, natalean/SS; 22 (UP), sh.el.photo/SS; 22 (CTR), Glenn Bartley/GI; 22 (LO), Mark Chappell/age fotostock; 23 (art), Kaya Dengel; 23 (pencils), Lukas Gojda/SS; 24, Callie Broaddus

Library of Congress Cataloging-in-Publication Data

Names: Szymanski, Jennifer, author.
Title: Ducks / by Jennifer Szymanski.
Description: Washington, DC : National Geographic Kids, 2018. | Series: National Geographic readers | Audience: Age 2-5. | Audience: Pre-school, excluding K.
Identifiers: LCCN 2017050027 (print) | LCCN 2017054894 (ebook) | ISBN 9781426332128 (ebook) | ISBN 9781426332135 (e-book + audio) | ISBN 9781426332104 (paperback) | ISBN 9781426332111 (hardcover)
Subjects: LCSH: Ducks--Juvenile literature. | BISAC: JUVENILE NONFICTION / Readers / Beginner. | JUVENILE NONFICTION / Animals / Birds. | JUVENILE NONFICTION / Animals / Ducks, Geese, etc.
Classification: LCC QL696.A52 (ebook) | LCC QL696.A52 S978 2018 (print) | DDC 598.4/1--dc23
LC record available at https://lccn.loc.gov/2017050027

Printed in the United States of America
18/WOR/1